Lit

That's Life

Day-to-Day Stories and Language Activities

INTRODUCTORY

TEACHER'S GUIDE

Ann Gianola

Instructor, San Diego Community College District
Instructor, University of San Diego English Language Academy
San Diego, California

New Readers Press

That's Life: Day-to-Day Stories and Language Activities
Teacher's Guide, Introductory Level
ISBN 978-1-56420-775-3

Copyright © 2008 New Readers Press
New Readers Press
A Publishing Division of ProLiteracy
1320 Jamesville Avenue, Syracuse, New York 13210
www.newreaderspress.com

Printed in the United States of America
9 8 7 6 5

All proceeds from the sale of New Readers Press materials
support literacy programs in the United States and worldwide.

Developmental Editor: Karen Davy
Creative Director: Andrea Woodbury
Production Specialist: Jeffrey R. Smith

Contents

Overview

That's Life is a series of four student books that provide stories and activities—each specifically designed for introductory, low-beginning, high-beginning, or low-intermediate English language learners. The primary goal is to provide entertaining and relevant reading material that corresponds to key thematic units often studied by ESL students:

1. People
2. Family
3. Transportation
4. Food
5. Health
6. Work
7. Shopping
8. Money
9. Community
10. Housing
11. Communication
12. School
13. Recreation
14. Technology
15. Civics

The topics in *That's Life* incorporate a wide variety of everyday situations, motivating students to read and develop fluency. The fifteen stories in each book portray diverse characters in interesting, often familiar, and sometimes amusing situations. In the Introductory Level of *That's Life,* students read about such characters as Liz, who briefly loses a child at the beach; Yuki, who wants to avoid standing in a long line at the post office; Vasu, who is awakened by a series of wrong telephone numbers; and Monica, who is delighted by a tax refund. The lessons are not designed to be sequential, so they can be taught in any order.

Although the main purpose of these books is to help students develop reading skills, they also include focused practice in reading comprehension, vocabulary reinforcement, speaking, listening, spelling, syntax, pronunciation, and other language areas.

The accompanying audio CD also provides a reading of each story, the dialog for each lesson, and prompts for the listening activities.

This Teacher's Guide contains notes for using the Introductory Level of *That's Life.* The notes for each lesson have two sections, Preview and Exercises. Preview lists the main themes of each story. It also lets students draw on prior experiences and share ideas or knowledge about issues in the story. In addition, Preview suggests warm-up activities, focusing on key concepts and vocabulary.

The Exercises section suggests ways to prepare for, carry out, and expand on exercises that follow the stories. The exercises are very easy to follow; these suggestions are provided to spark additional ideas.

Using *That's Life,* Introductory Level

Preview Activities

The illustrations that accompany each story are useful prompts for warm-up or preview activities. They can help create interest in the story, provide a starting point for discussion, and help introduce new vocabulary. They also help students reflect on personal experiences. Have students look at the illustrations, particularly the one that precedes the story. Encourage students to describe what they see, or prompt them with questions (e.g., "What do you see? Is this a man or a woman? Where is he or she? What do you think is the problem?"). If possible, have students use the illustration to guess what the story is about and make predictions about what will happen. Keep in mind that at this very low level, students' responses may be only phrases or single words. For these learners, using words to identify objects in pictures is an important first step in vocabulary building.

As you introduce or review vocabulary, write the words on the board and explain them through pictures (including the story illustration) or, when possible, real items. Encourage students to explain words they already know.

Stories

To present the stories, you can have students first listen to the audio CD one or more times to get a sense of the story line. Or you may prefer to have students initially follow the written text while listening to the recording. Pose a general comprehension question to focus students' listening and reading. On repetitions of the story, you may want to add other, more specific questions.

A primary goal at this level is to give students repeated exposure to key words and sentence patterns. Sentences from the stories are recycled consistently in follow-up exercises. The word-for-word repetition of vocabulary and phrasing is intentional, providing valuable practice for students.

Complete the story.

In the Introductory Level, each story is followed by a cloze exercise. Use this to integrate the four language skills: reading, writing, listening, and speaking. This activity presents the story in paragraph form. It requires students to refer to the story, reading to find specific words and then seeing where the words fit into sentences. Encourage students to say missing words and read aloud the completed story. Ask students to listen to their partners and check for correct pronunciation.

Comprehension Activities

At the Introductory Level, there are Yes/No statements following the cloze activity. Encourage students to provide correct statements when an answer is No. These activities can be done either orally or in writing.

Vocabulary Exercises

These word-based or picture-based exercises help students reinforce their understanding of words from the story and expand their vocabulary with related words. Encourage students to discuss the vocabulary in their own words, use it in new sentences, or comment on the sentences. Word-based vocabulary exercises are organized in grammatical categories of verbs, nouns, adjectives, and prepositions.

Dialogs

Each lesson contains a dialog based on the story. These dialogs, which can also be heard on the audio CD, model key interactions from the story. Have the students listen before reading the dialog. Play the audio CD several times if necessary. Check comprehension and discuss the content. Then play the audio again one or more times. You can also read the dialog from the student book; stop after each line and have students repeat what was said. This activity prepares students to act out the dialog and provides useful pronunciation practice. Students can then practice with partners, using their books if necessary. If possible, encourage students to improvise their own conversations based on the dialog and to create new conversations on related topics. For additional practice, write these new conversations on the board for students to copy and say. Dialogs can also create opportunities for role-play activities.

Listening Exercises

Listening exercises, at this level, generally focus on understanding different actions within the story. Most of the listening exercises are picture-based, requiring students to number the picture that best illustrates the listening prompt. Other listening exercises have students either transcribe a number or discriminate between two telephone numbers or dollar amounts. The prompts for these exercises are on the audio CD. They are also printed at the end of the student book so that you can read them if the audio is not available or have students prompt each other. The printed prompts also let students check their answers.

Missing Letters

The missing-letter activity gives students additional spelling practice, focusing on either a missing vowel or consonant. After students complete the activity, rewrite the words on the board with a blank line for a different vowel or consonant. Work up to having the students spell the words independently.

Same Sound / Unscramble the sentences

The Same Sound exercises focus on pronunciation and identifying other words from the story with common vowel sounds. Assist students, if necessary, by reading the first word containing the target vowel sound. Ask students to then choose two of the three word choices containing the same vowel sound. Also, encourage students to read the options aloud to strengthen their auditory discrimination skills.

In Unscramble the Sentences, students increase their knowledge of English syntax by arranging different word sequences and deciding which one is correct. In this activity, students may also be motivated to reread the text for assistance in correctly reordering words into sentences from the story.

About You

This activity allows students to personalize various events in the stories and reflect on their own experience with a specific subject. The exercise also gives students who are able an opportunity to share additional thoughts and information on a topic. Encourage students to form questions for practice with partners (e.g., "Do you sometimes go to the beach?" "Do you sometimes get lost?").

Lesson Notes

Lesson 1
Lost at the Beach (pp. 4–9)
Theme: People
Preview

Details in this story offer the opportunity to teach or review vocabulary for physical descriptions, clothing, colors, and emotions.

Discuss places where large numbers of people go and where a child, in particular, can get lost (e.g., beach, shopping mall, sporting event, amusement park). Teach or review some emotions a parent can feel when a child is lost (e.g., worried, anxious, upset, nervous). Brainstorm a list of people who can help find a lost child (e.g., lifeguard, police officer, security guard).

Encourage students to practice the names and ages of their children or other people in their homes (e.g., "My son's name is Dominic. He's five years old." "My roommate's name is Gita. She's twenty-four years old." "My husband's name is Antonio. He's thirty-two years old.").

Teach or review names of colors, clothing, and accessories. Encourage students to give a brief physical description of someone in the class (e.g., "Mario has black hair and brown eyes."). If possible, ask students to describe what that classmate is wearing (e.g., "Mario is wearing a blue shirt. He's wearing a red cap. He's wearing glasses."). Practice describing people in pictures or other students in the classroom.

Introduce or review other key vocabulary as needed (e.g., beach, worried, daughter, lost, lifeguard, describe, freckles, hat, binoculars, bathing suit, behind).

Exercises

Mia Encourage students to use the adjectives that describe these nouns (e.g., *brown* hair, *blue* eyes, *green* bathing suit, *big* hat).

Talking to a Lifeguard Elicit responses about other people who can be lost (e.g., niece, grandson, friend). Have students work in pairs to describe their partners as the lost person.

About You In number 1, have students name locations near water where people in your community go for recreation. Ask about whether or not lifeguards are on duty.

Lesson 2
A Family Photo (pp. 10–15)
Theme: Family
Preview

Details in this story offer the opportunity to teach or review vocabulary for the family and for defining different relationships.

Teach or review the names for family members. If possible, use pictures that show connections between individuals (e.g., mother, grandfather, aunt, granddaughter). Indicate people by *pointing* as demonstrated in the story.

Ask students about family photos they have. Elicit responses about the people in these photos (e.g., mother, father, daughter, husband). Encourage students to discuss where they keep these photos (e.g., on a wall, in a photo album, in a wallet, on a shelf, on a computer disc).

Discuss ways to keep in touch with family or friends who live far away (e.g., letters, e-mail, telephone calls, visits). Teach or review the word *miss* and model a statement and follow-up question for practice in pairs (e.g., "I miss my mother. Who do you miss?").

Teach or review the names of common household pets. Ask students about their pets (e.g., "I have a cat. Her name is Daisy. My neighbor has a dog. His name is Pepper."). Ask students if they have any photos of their pets.

Introduce or review other key vocabulary as needed (e.g., photo, family, son, mother, grandmother, father, grandfather, sister, aunt, brother, uncle, dog, remember, visit, miss).

Exercises
If possible, encourage students to bring in photos of their own families for additional practice in explaining relationships (e.g., "This is Ivan. He's my brother. He's my mother's son. He's my daughter's uncle.").

Talking to Berto Consider using students' photos to practice the questions modeled in the dialog. Have each partner ask questions (e.g., "Who is he? Who is she? Who are they?").

About You In number 3, elicit responses from students about how often they visit their families (e.g., "I visit my family once a year." "I visit my family every two years." "I never visit my family.").

Lesson 3
Seeing Signs (pp. 16–21)
Theme: Transportation
Preview

Details in this story offer the opportunity to teach or review vocabulary for reading and understanding traffic signs and the habits of a good driver.

If possible, use pictures to teach or review the pronunciation and meaning of common traffic signs, especially signs for *Stop, Speed Limit,* and *No U-turn* as they appear in the story. For Speed Limit, check what students already know about speed limits on main streets and freeways, in school zones and residential areas, etc.

Elicit responses about things good drivers do (e.g., watch the road, read signs, drive the correct speed limit). Discuss consequences of not being a good driver (e.g., "You can have an accident." "You can get a ticket.").

Teach or review the concept of getting a ticket and talk about other reasons people can receive them (e.g., driving too fast, driving through a red light or Stop sign). Have students think about how a police officer stops a driver (e.g., siren, flashing light, message on loudspeaker, hand signal). Think about things that can distract a driver (e.g., cell phone, reading billboards, loud music, conversation with someone else, turning around).

Discuss gas stations as places to get gas. Elicit other services that may be available at a gas station (e.g., oil change, car wash, car repair, convenience store). Talk about names and locations of gas stations in your community.

Introduce or review other key vocabulary as needed (e.g., driving, sign, driver, speedometer, gas station, gas, police officer, sorry).

Exercises

Signs Use pictures and have students identify other traffic signs and their meanings (e.g., "That is a One-way sign. You have to drive in one direction.").

Talking to a Police Officer Discuss other violations a police officer can mention (e.g., "You can't park here." "You can't enter here." "You can't turn right here.").

About You Talk about other tickets people can get (e.g., speeding, parking, jaywalking). If possible, elicit information about fines associated with different violations.

Lesson 4
Apples On Sale (pp. 22–27)
Theme: Food
Preview

Details in this story offer the opportunity to teach or review vocabulary for fruit and other foods and for reading and understanding supermarket advertisements.

If possible, bring in some supermarket advertisements. Ask students if they look at ads for supermarkets or other food stores. Ask where they find these ads (e.g., in the newspaper, in the mail).

As a whole class, brainstorm a list of fruits. Encourage students to ask one another which fruits they like. Have them report back (e.g., "I like grapes. Joaquin likes pears."). Elicit responses about the price per pound of apples. Teach or review the meaning of *a good price* as it appears in the story. Identify fruits that are generally less expensive.

Ask about stores in your community where students buy food. Ask which stores are less expensive. Ask them if they write a shopping list at home and if they sometimes forget an item they need. Model the past tense as it appears in the story (e.g., "Last week, I forgot to buy potatoes."). Discuss other items that students routinely buy.

Introduce or review other key vocabulary as needed (e.g., home, supermarket, ad, apples, on sale, pound, price, bananas, cheap, shopping cart, things, money, unpack, forgot).

Exercises

In a Supermarket Hold up other pictures of food and find out whether or not students buy these items and what is a good price for them.

Talking About a Supermarket Ad Encourage students to practice this dialog using non-count nouns (e.g., chicken, rice, coffee). Have them practice with partners (e.g., "Chicken is on sale. How much is it?").

About You In number 3, ask students about how much they spend on food at the supermarket or other food stores.

Lesson 5
A Busy Doctor (pp. 28–33)
Theme: Health
Preview

Details in this story offer the opportunity to teach or review vocabulary for parts of the body, expressing symptoms of an illness or injury, and medical exams.

Discuss going to a doctor for medical treatment. Elicit responses from students about where they can get medical care in your community. Brainstorm reasons why people go to a doctor (e.g., "They are sick." "They are injured." "They need a checkup."). Ask if these offices, clinics, or hospitals are typically *busy*. Ask how long students may *wait* to see a doctor (e.g., ten minutes, thirty minutes, one hour).

Discuss activities that are performed in routine medical exams. Explain the difference between *look in* and *listen to* as they appear in the story. Identify the body parts that a doctor *looks in* (e.g., mouth, ears, eyes) and *listens to* (e.g., heart and lungs). Elicit responses about other things that happen in a medical exam (e.g., check weight, take blood pressure, take body temperature).

Demonstrate having difficulty walking. Point to your foot and teach or review the expression "My foot hurts." Practice the expression using other appropriate body parts (e.g., leg, arm, throat, shoulder). Introduce other ways to express symptoms of a problem (e.g., "I have a pain in my _____." "I have a sore _____."). Also, teach or review the expression "Everything is fine." Explain that it means there are no physical problems. Teach or review "Everything *isn't* fine" to indicate that there is a problem.

Introduce or review other key vocabulary as needed (e.g., busy, people, waiting, examining room, mouth, ears, eyes, stethoscope, heart, lungs, fine, healthy, next year).

Exercises

Body Parts Use pictures to identify and practice names for other body parts.

Talking to the Doctor Encourage students to substitute a different body part for the *foot* used in the dialog (e.g., "My elbow hurts." "My throat hurts." "My knee hurts.").

About You In number 4, elicit responses from students about how often they go to the doctor (e.g., "I go to the doctor once a year." "I never go to the doctor." "I go to the doctor when I'm sick." "I go to the doctor when my child is sick.").

Lesson 6
A Bump on the Head (pp. 34–39)
Theme: Work
Preview

Details in this story offer the opportunity to teach or review vocabulary for injuries and practicing safety at work.

Using pictures, show students examples of protective clothing or devices that some people use at work (e.g., hard hat, safety glasses, latex gloves, safety boots, particle mask). Elicit responses for the body part that various items protect (e.g., "A hard hat protects your head." "Safety glasses protect your eyes.").

Encourage students to name occupations where workers wear special protective clothing or devices (e.g., construction worker, laboratory worker, custodian, carpenter, electrician, firefighter). Discuss why these workers wear these items (e.g., "A construction worker wears a hard hat to protect his head.").

Teach or review the word *box*. Ask students if they have any boxes at home. Brainstorm a list of items students keep in a closet at home. Demonstrate how some things can *fall off* a *shelf* and *hit* someone on the head. Teach or review the expression "Ouch!" as a response to pain.

On the board, draw a picture of a head with a *bump* on it. Ask students what they do for a minor injury of this kind (e.g., ice, pain reliever). Ask students about signs that indicate a more serious head injury and the need for medical treatment (e.g., bad headache, imbalance, vomiting, unconsciousness).

Discuss potential hazards people can have at work (e.g., exposure to infections, burns, hearing loss, eye injury, lung injury). Elicit responses about clothing or devices that can protect workers from these problems.

Introduce or review other key vocabulary as needed (e.g., construction worker, leaving, closet, jacket, box, falls off, shelf, bump, okay, ice, work, arrives, boss, hard hat, protect).

Exercises

On Mike's Head In addition to ice, discuss things students may have at home that can be helpful in treating minor injuries (e.g., antibiotic ointment, bandages, antiseptic, pain medication).

Talking with the Boss Encourage students to substitute other protective clothes or devices for the hard hat and explain its function (e.g., "They're safety goggles. Wear these to protect your eyes.").

About You In number 4, ask students about what they wear to work. Model ways to ask for protective clothing or devices when safety is an issue (e.g., "This is a hazardous chemical. I need a respirator.").

Lesson 7
A Cheap Umbrella
(pp. 40–45)
Theme: Shopping
Preview

Details in this story offer the opportunity to teach or review vocabulary for shopping at a yard sale and price bargaining.

Teach or review the words *yard sale* and ask students if they ever buy or sell things at a yard sale. Ask about items that are often found at yard sales (e.g., clothing, furniture, dishes, toys). Elicit responses about other places where people buy and sell things informally (e.g., garage sale, swap meet, street fair). Ask students if they feel *curious* when they see a yard sale. Ask them if they like to find something *cheap*.

Review numbers, terms for money, and how to read and say prices. Review colors and have students identify items in the classroom by color (e.g., yellow shirt, white cup, blue notebook).

Elicit responses from students about the cost of a new umbrella. If possible, bring in an umbrella. Tell students you are selling the umbrella for $4. Encourage students to bargain with you for a cheaper price (e.g., "How about $2?" "Will you take $3?" "Is $2.50 okay?").

Discuss culturally different attitudes about bargaining. Make sure students understand when it is acceptable in the U.S. (e.g., at a yard sale) and when it is usually not (e.g., in a department store or supermarket).

Introduce or review other key vocabulary as needed (e.g., neighbor, yard sale, outside, curious, cheap, black, umbrella, happy, use, sold, paid).

Exercises

At the Yard Sale Issue words for or pictures of random items (e.g., table, coat, toaster, bicycle). Tell students they represent things for sale at a yard sale. Elicit responses about the price of each item. Encourage students to bargain with one another in pairs or small groups. If possible, have them report back using the past tense (e.g., "I sold May a table. She paid $35.").

Talking at a Yard Sale Substitute another item for the umbrella and vary the price exchanges.

About You In numbers 1 and 2, encourage students to talk about real items they buy or sell at yard sales or similar venues.

Lesson 8
Bus Fare (pp. 46–51)
Theme: Money
Preview

Details in this story offer the opportunity to teach or review vocabulary for money and counting coins.

Teach or review the names and monetary value for *quarter, dime,* and *nickel* as they appear in the story. Explain the meaning of *dollars* and *cents, bills* and *coins.* If possible, show or pass around real coins. If students are interested, also include explanations of penny, half dollar, and one-dollar coins.

Ask students where they carry coins (e.g., pocket, coin purse, wallet, hand). Ask students how they can exchange bills for coins (e.g., ask someone, buy something in a store, use a change machine).

Ask students if they take the bus in your community. Teach or review the word *fare.* Ask what the bus fare is and how they pay it (e.g., coins, bills, bus pass, token). Find out if the driver takes bills or coins. Ask students where the nearest bus stop is.

Point out examples of buttons on clothing. Demonstrate how a button can *fall off* clothing. Act out putting a loose button in your pocket. Then act out *reaching* back into that pocket to retrieve coins or other objects.

Introduce or review other key vocabulary as needed (e.g., bus stop, button, falls off, shirt, pocket, bus, reaches, fare, coins, machine, bills, quarters, dimes, nickels, dollars, cents, bus driver).

Exercises

Coins in Jim's Pocket Have students work individually or in pairs to calculate the dollars or cents amount of the coins they are carrying. Encourage students to count out change as demonstrated in the story.

Talking to the Bus Driver Vary the bus fare (e.g., one dollar, three dollars, two dollars and fifty cents).

About You In number 1, ask students where they take the bus (e.g., to work, to school, to the store, home).

Lesson 9
Buying Stamps (pp. 52–57)
Theme: Community
Preview

Details in this story offer the opportunity to teach or review vocabulary for buying stamps at the post office.

Ask students how they buy stamps (e.g., at the post office, on the Internet, through the mail, at a store). For students who go to the post office to buy stamps, elicit responses as to whether they stand in line or buy stamps from the machines.

Ask about students' preference for stamps (e.g., flags, birds, flowers, holidays, famous people). Have students practice questions to request a specific stamp (e.g., "Do you have any flag stamps?" "Do you have any bird stamps?" "Do you have any flower stamps?").

Ask students about places where people routinely *stand in line* (e.g., post office, store, bank, train station). Elicit responses about how they feel standing in line (e.g., bored, angry, tired). Get opinions about how long a person can expect to stand in line at the post office (e.g., five minutes, ten minutes, twenty minutes).

Ask students about other reasons people stand in line at the post office (e.g., sending a package, asking them to hold mail, sending letters of different weights). Then elicit responses about other ways to do these things (e.g., going to a postal store, using the Internet, using a postal scale to determine postage).

Introduce or review other key vocabulary as needed (e.g., post office, stamps, birds, line, machines, gets out, looks into, different, postal clerk).

Exercises

At the Post Office Ask students about other items they buy from machines (e.g., stamps, laundry detergent, snacks, public transportation tickets).

Talking to a Postal Clerk Encourage students to change the location of the stamp machines (e.g., "They're over there on the left." "They're down the hall." "They're next to the doors."). Have partners substitute bird stamps for other stamps (e.g., "Do you have any holiday stamps?").

About You In number 1, encourage students to talk about the value of stamps they buy. Ask if they buy first-class letter postage or other stamps. Ask, "How much does it cost to send letters to your native country?"

Lesson 10
Moving Day (pp. 58–63)
Theme: Housing
Preview

Details in this story offer the opportunity to teach or review vocabulary for housing and furniture as well as provide practice with prepositions.

Teach or review the names of the objects in the story and the prepositions that refer to their locations. If possible, use classroom furniture and label it as *chair, sofa,* and *TV* as they appear in the story. Arrange different configurations of furniture, putting the chair *next to, across from, to the right,* and *to the left* of the sofa or *in front of* the TV. Pick up a chair and pretend that it is *heavy.* Sit *on* a chair and demonstrate feeling *tired.*

Ask students where they have a chair at home and elicit responses (e.g., "The chair is next to the window." "The chair is across from the TV." "The chair is to the right of the table."). Brainstorm a list of objects at home that are heavy (e.g., refrigerator, bed, table).

Introduce or review other key vocabulary as needed (e.g., moving, apartment, carrying, there, here, no).

Exercises

Things in an Apartment Make a list of other furniture or items that are commonly found in the living room. Use a picture of a living room to practice names and locations of objects (e.g., "The pillow is on the sofa. The lamp is to the left of the chair.").

Talking on Moving Day Encourage students to substitute other objects for the chair in the dialog (e.g., lamp, coffee table, plant, mirror, bookcase).

About You In number 2, ask students to describe a chair at home or bring in pictures of chairs for the class to describe (e.g., "It's green. It's heavy. It's comfortable. It's big. It's old.").

Lesson 11
The Wrong Number
(pp. 64–69)
Theme: Communication
Preview

Details in this story offer the opportunity to teach or review vocabulary for getting a wrong number on the telephone.

Teach or review the verb *rings*. Demonstrate a telephone ringing. Ask students how they answer the phone (e.g., "Hello?"). Elicit responses about what a caller says (e.g., "May I please speak to Ana?" "Is Ana there?"). Ask students if they ever get wrong numbers and what they say to the person calling (e.g., "You have the wrong number." "There is no Ana here."). Brainstorm things the caller can say (e.g., "Sorry to bother you." "Sorry. I have the wrong number.").

Ask students if they feel annoyed when they get a wrong number. Clarify the meanings of *pick up* and *hang up*. Ask students if they talk to the caller or simply hang up. Ask students how they feel when the phone rings when they are sleeping (e.g., angry, scared, annoyed). Ask what they do (e.g., pick it up, don't pick it up, let the answering machine get it). Ask about other unwanted telephone calls (e.g., telemarketers, automated calls).

Teach or review the numbers one through ten. Practice reciting random seven-digit phone numbers. Say or elicit the area code or codes in your community.

Introduce or review other key vocabulary as needed (e.g., sleeping, telephone, rings, wakes up, picks up, speak, wrong number, hangs up, again, sorry, bother, closes, eyes, angry).

Exercises

The Telephone Ask students about how often their telephones ring and when the phone rings most often (in the morning, in the afternoon, in the evening, at night).

Answering the Telephone Encourage students to change the name and phone number for extra practice.

About You In number 2, ask students who in their homes usually picks up the phone when it is ringing (e.g., daughter, husband, brother-in-law, mother).

Lesson 12
School Supplies (pp. 70–75)
Theme: School
Preview

Details in this story offer the opportunity to teach or review vocabulary for school supplies.

Teach or review the meaning of *school supplies*. Show examples of school supplies in the classroom (e.g., pencil, pen, scissors, tape). Then elicit responses about school supplies children often need (e.g., pencils, paper, notebook). Think about things for younger children (e.g., crayons) and older children (e.g., calculator). Ask your adult students about school supplies they need for your class.

Ask students where they shop for school supplies in your community (e.g., office supply store, department store, pharmacy, supermarket, warehouse store). Ask students which places are the most convenient or inexpensive. Encourage students to list other things children need at the beginning of the school year (e.g., clothes, shoes, books).

Teach or review general information about ages and corresponding grade levels (e.g., "A five-year-old goes to kindergarten. A six-year-old goes to first grade."). Teach or review the months of the year. Mention that school usually begins in *September* and ends in *June*. Ask if the school year is similar in students' native countries. Elicit responses about whether or not children are *excited* about beginning the school year.

Introduce or review other key vocabulary as needed (e.g., excited, school supplies, father, store, shopping basket, paper, pencils, erasers, notebook, ruler, scissors, full, teacher, July, September).

Exercises

School Supplies Encourage students to expand the list of school supplies and include items not mentioned in the story (e.g., poster board, glue, markers).

Buying School Supplies Substitute another school supply for paper (e.g., "Do I need more tape?" "Do I need more markers?").

About You In number 4, talk about the months that English classes start at your site (e.g., September, January, June).

Lesson 13
The Park (pp. 76–81)
Theme: Recreation
Preview

Details in this story offer the opportunity to teach or review vocabulary for going to the park.

Ask students about the names and locations of some parks in your community. Encourage students to talk about various things in the park (e.g., playground, grass, trees, fountain, garden, museum, restroom, bench, pond, basketball court).

Talk about areas that are particularly appealing for young children, like a playground. Teach or review the names of some common things in a playground as they appear in the story (e.g., swing, slide, monkey bars, sand). Also, explain the meaning of the prepositions in the story (e.g., down, through, behind, on, in).

Ask students if they ever take young children to the park and, if so, what activities they do with them. Ask how long they typically spend there (e.g., thirty minutes, one hour, two hours, all day). Consider acting out the action verbs in the story (e.g., runs, pushes, catches, helps, digs). Teach or review the feeling *tired* and the meaning of the expression "Let's go."

Introduce or review other key vocabulary as needed (e.g., son, afternoon, park, hill, trees, hour, time, home, tired, carry).

Exercises

Things at the Park Brainstorm other equipment that may be in a playground (e.g., merry-go-round, jungle gym, seesaw).

Talking at the Park Use another relationship as substitute for Mommy (e.g., "But Daddy is very tired." "But Grandma is very tired." "But Nanny is very tired.").

About You In number 3, elicit responses about how students can help a child at the park (e.g., "I can watch a child." "I can carry a child." "I can play with a child.").

Lesson 14
At 1:00 A.M. (pp. 82–87)
Theme: Technology
Preview

Details in this story offer the opportunity to teach or review vocabulary for using a remote to operate a CD player and a TV.

Teach or review the language for telling time. Clarify *A.M.* and *P.M.*, especially the time 1:00 A.M. in the story. Ask students what they're doing at 1:00 A.M. (e.g., sleeping, watching TV, working). Ask students what time they go to bed. Ask if they sometimes *can't sleep*. Ask what they do when they can't sleep (e.g., listen to music, read, watch TV, drink warm milk).

Elicit responses about how students *listen to music* (e.g., CD, radio, computer). Ask, "Do you have a CD player? Do you have a remote to operate it?" Ask about other remotes they may have at home (TV, DVD, VCR). Ask them where they keep remotes (e.g., in a drawer, on the nightstand, on a table, under the sofa). Ask if they ever confuse one remote with another.

Teach or review the term *Power button*. Ask students what they do when they *push* the Power button and the remote doesn't work (e.g., put in new batteries, turn the appliance on manually, buy a new remote). Ask students if they have batteries at home for remotes or other things that need batteries.

Ask students if they ever watch movies on TV. Elicit responses about movies they like. Ask if they watch other late-night programs on TV.

Introduce or review other key vocabulary as needed (e.g., sleep, music, favorite, CD player, relaxes, reaches, remote, nightstand, pushes, Power button, nothing, batteries, opens, drawer, two, wrong, movie).

Exercises

In Jing's Room Ask students about additional items that use batteries. If possible, bring in some examples of batteries. Discuss the sizes and the places you may use them (smoke detector, flashlight, portable radio, toy, watch).

Talking at Home Substitute another item that uses batteries. Vary the number of batteries as well as the location (e.g., "They're in the cabinet." "They're on the shelf." "They're in the closet." "They're in the dresser.").

About You In number 2, elicit additional responses about things that relax students (e.g., "Exercise relaxes me." "Reading relaxes me." "A warm bath relaxes me.").

Lesson 15
Income Tax (pp. 88–93)
Theme: Civics
Preview

Details in this story offer the opportunity to teach or review vocabulary for getting assistance to pay income taxes.

Ask students if they have jobs and where those jobs are. Ask, "Do you receive a W-2 form (wage and tax statement) from your employer in January for the previous year?" Talk about the information that is on a W-2 form (e.g., earnings, taxes). If possible, use a sample of a W-2 form and explain the information on it.

Explain the meaning of *federal* and *state*. Ask students if they file federal and state income tax returns. Explain the meaning of a *Taxpayer Assistance Center*. Inform students that it's a place people can go for free help in *filling out* federal and state income tax returns. Remind students about the filing date of April 15th. Point to that date on a calendar if necessary.

Teach or review the word *refund* as it appears in the story. Explain that a refund means that the government *owes* you money and sends you a check. Ask students about things they *need* money for (e.g., food, rent, transportation, school).

Introduce or review other key vocabulary as needed (e.g., home, mail, W-2 form, job, restaurant, earnings, taxes, last year, fill out, copy, file, refund, government, owes).

Exercises

About Income Tax Research the name, address, and hours of operation for a Taxpayer Assistance Center in your community. Find out how people qualify for free income tax assistance.

Talking at the Taxpayer Assistance Center Help students with other questions they may have for a staff member at a Taxpayer Assistance Center (e.g., "How can I file returns for previous years?" "How much money do I owe the government?").

About You In number 2, ask students who they get help from (e.g., accountant, tax preparation service, friend, family member, Taxpayer Assistance Center).

Answer Key

Lesson 1

Complete the story. (p. 5)

1. worried
2. lost
3. lifeguard
4. daughter
5. eyes
6. binoculars
7. green
8. behind

Check (✔) *Yes* or *No*. (p. 6)

1. Yes
2. No
3. Yes
4. No
5. No
6. Yes
7. No
8. Yes
9. No
10. Yes

Mia (p. 6)

1. hat
2. freckles
3. eyes
4. hair
5. bathing suit

Complete the sentences. (p. 7)

1. runs
2. describes
3. has
4. looks
5. sees
6. is

Listening (p. 8)

a. 4
b. 1
c. 5
d. 6
e. 3
f. 2

Missing Letters (p. 9)

1. lost
2. lifeguard
3. behind
4. describes
5. freckles
6. bathing
7. beach
8. worried
9. binoculars

Same Sound (p. 9)

2. through, suit
3. lost, daughter
4. lifeguard, describes
5. freckles, seven

Lesson 2

Complete the story. (p. 11)

1. photo
2. son
3. family
4. grandmother
5. grandfather
6. aunt
7. uncle
8. visit

Check (✔) *Yes* or *No*. (p. 12)

1. Yes
2. No
3. Yes
4. No
5. Yes
6. No
7. Yes
8. Yes
9. No
10. No

The Photo (p. 12)

1. grandfather
2. grandmother
3. dog
4. uncle
5. aunt

Complete the sentences. (p. 13)

1. son
2. mother
3. father
4. sister
5. brother

Listening (p. 14)

a. 3
b. 6
c. 1
d. 5
e. 2
f. 4

Missing Letters (p. 15)

1. ph<u>o</u>to
2. thr<u>ee</u>
3. fami<u>l</u>y
4. m<u>o</u>ther
5. smil<u>e</u>s
6. s<u>i</u>ster
7. a<u>u</u>nt
8. f<u>a</u>ther
9. po<u>i</u>nts

Unscramble the sentences. (p. 15)

1. Dina is looking at a photo.
2. Her son Berto wants to see it, too.
3. Dina points to her father.

Lesson 3

Complete the story. (p. 17)

1. Stop
2. car
3. Speed
4. speedometer
5. gas
6. U-turn

7. police
8. sign

Check (✔) *Yes* or *No.* (p. 18)

1. No
2. Yes
3. Yes
4. Yes
5. No
6. No
7. Yes
8. No
9. No
10. Yes

Signs (p. 18)

1. No U-turn
2. Stop
3. Speed Limit

Complete the sentences. (p. 19)

1. sees
2. stops
3. looks
4. needs
5. makes
6. doesn't see

Listening (p. 20)

a. 5
b. 2
c. 1
d. 3
e. 6
f. 4

Missing Letters (p. 21)

1. si<u>g</u>n
2. s<u>t</u>reet
3. s<u>p</u>eed
4. hou<u>r</u>
5. dri<u>v</u>er
6. li<u>m</u>it
7. U-tur<u>n</u>
8. acro<u>ss</u>
9. poli<u>c</u>e

Same Sound (p. 21)

2. limit, ticket

3. sees, needs

4. lake, station

5. stops, problem

Lesson 4

Complete the story. (p. 23)

1. supermarket

2. cents

3. price

4. apples

5. cheap

6. bananas

7. money

8. food

Check (✔) *Yes* or *No*. (p. 24)

1. Yes

2. No

3. No

4. Yes

5. Yes

6. No

7. Yes

8. No

9. Yes

10. No

In a Supermarket (p. 24)

1. bananas

2. shopping cart

3. apples

Complete the sentences. (p. 25)

1. puts

2. buys

3. spends

4. goes

5. unpacks

6. says

Listening (p. 26)

a. 3

b. 2

c. 6

d. 1

e. 5

f. 4

Missing Letters (p. 27)

1. fo_o_d

2. che_a_p

3. sup_e_rmarket

4. h_o_me

5. ban_a_nas

6. m_o_ney

7. po_u_nd

8. pr_i_ce

9. appl_e_s

Unscramble the sentences. (p. 27)

1. She is looking at a supermarket ad.

2. They are 39 cents a pound.

3. She puts bananas in her shopping cart.

Lesson 5

Complete the story. (p. 29)

1. busy

2. waiting

3. mouth

4. looks

5. heart

6. listens

7. healthy

8. fine

Check (✔) *Yes* or *No*. (p. 30)

1. Yes

2. No

3. Yes

4. No

5. Yes

6. No

7. No

8. Yes

9. Yes

10. No

Body Parts (p. 30)

1. ear

2. lung

3. foot

4. eye

5. mouth

6. heart

Complete the sentences. (p. 31)

1. looks in

2. listens to

3. looks in

4. looks in

5. listens to

Listening (p. 32)

a. 3

b. 4

c. 2

d. 6

e. 1

f. 5

Missing Letters (p. 33)

1. eyes

2. mouth

3. examining

4. hurts

5. waiting

6. stethoscope

7. everything

8. listens

9. people

Same Sound (p. 33)

2. people, she

3. I'll, eyes

4. puts, foot

5. healthy, says

Lesson 6

Complete the story. (p. 35)

1. work

2. closet

3. box

4. head

5. bump

6. ice

7. hat

8. protect

Check (✔) *Yes* or *No*. (p. 36)

1. Yes

2. Yes

3. No

4. No

5. Yes

6. Yes

7. No

8. No

9. Yes

10. No

On Mike's Head (p. 36)

1. hard hat

2. bump

3. ice

Complete the sentences. (p. 37)

1. falls

2. hits

3. has

4. hurts

5. puts

6. gives

Listening (p. 38)

a. 4

b. 2

c. 5

d. 1

e. 6

f. 3

Missing Letters (p. 39)

1. bump

2. protect

3. jacket

4. closet

5. worker

6. shelf

7. construction

8. ice

9. leaving

Same Sound (p. 39)

2. I, right

3. boss, falls

4. jacket, thanks

5. hurts, worker

Lesson 7

Complete the story. (p. 41)

1. yard
2. for
3. sale
4. cheap
5. umbrella
6. How
7. gives
8. sold

Check (✔) *Yes* or *No*. (p. 42)

1. Yes
2. No
3. Yes
4. No
5. No
6. Yes
7. No
8. Yes
9. Yes
10. No

At the Yard Sale (p. 42)

1. dollars
2. neighbor
3. umbrella

Complete the sentences. (p. 43)

1. yard
2. curious
3. cheap
4. black
5. nice
6. happy

Listening (p. 44)

A. a. 3
   b. 4
   c. 1
   d. 2

B. 2. 10
   3. 5
   4. 8

5. 3
6. 6
7. 9
8. 1
9. 7
10. 2
11. 15
12. 11

Missing Letters (p. 45)

1. cu<u>r</u>ious
2. so<u>l</u>d
3. yar<u>d</u>
4. c<u>h</u>eap
5. neighbor
6. dol<u>l</u>ars
7. some<u>t</u>hing
8. um<u>b</u>rella
9. out<u>s</u>ide

Unscramble the sentences. (p. 45)

1. Sarita's neighbor Gus is having a yard sale.
2. He has many things for sale outside.
3. Sarita picks up a black umbrella.

Lesson 8

Complete the story. (p. 47)

1. button
2. pocket
3. bus
4. fare
5. quarters
6. dimes
7. nickels
8. coins

Check (✔) *Yes* or *No*. (p. 48)

1. Yes
2. No
3. Yes
4. No
5. No
6. Yes
7. No
8. Yes
9. No
10. Yes

Coins in Jim's Pocket (p. 48)

1. dimes   thirty cents
2. nickels   twenty cents
3. quarters   one dollar and fifty cents

Complete the sentences. (p. 49)

1. dollars
2. quarters
3. cents
4. dimes
5. nickels
6. coins

Listening (p. 50)

a. 4
b. 1
c. 3
d. 6
e. 5
f. 2

Missing Letters (p. 51)

1. machine
2. quarters
3. pocket
4. fare
5. button
6. dimes
7. coins
8. nickels
9. reaches

Same Sound (p. 51)

2. coming, button
3. pocket, dollar
4. fifty, nickels
5. reaches, three

Lesson 9

Complete the story. (p. 53)

1. post
2. office
3. stamps
4. line
5. machines
6. bird

7. clerk
8. stand

Check (✔) *Yes* or *No*. (p. 54)

1. Yes
2. Yes
3. No
4. Yes
5. No
6. Yes
7. No
8. No
9. Yes
10. No

At the Post Office (p. 54)

1. line
2. stamp machine
3. stamps

Complete the sentences. (p. 55)

1. likes
2. stands
3. sees
4. gets out
5. looks
6. doesn't see

Listening (p. 56)

a. 4
b. 6
c. 5
d. 1
e. 3
f. 2

Missing Letters (p. 57)

1. clerk
2. machines
3. standing
4. stamps
5. different
6. line
7. post office
8. long
9. birds

Unscramble the sentences. (p. 57)

1. Yuki likes the stamps with birds on them.
2. She is standing in a long line.
3. Yuki sees some stamp machines.

Lesson 10

Complete the story. (p. 59)

1. moving
2. chair
3. puts
4. across
5. right
6. tired
7. heavy
8. sofa

Check (✔) Yes or No. (p. 60)

1. No
2. No
3. Yes
4. No
5. Yes
6. Yes
7. No
8. No
9. Yes
10. Yes

Things in an Apartment (p. 60)

1. TV
2. sofa
3. chair

Complete the sentences. (p. 61)

1. into
2. next
3. across
4. right
5. in front
6. on

Listening (p. 62)

a. 6
b. 3
c. 1
d. 2
e. 5
f. 4

Missing Letters (p. 63)

1. he<u>a</u>vy
2. apartm<u>e</u>nt
3. m<u>o</u>ving
4. s<u>o</u>fa
5. r<u>i</u>ght
6. tir<u>e</u>d
7. acr<u>o</u>ss
8. cha<u>i</u>r
9. p<u>u</u>ts

Unscramble the sentences. (p. 63)

1. Mark is carrying a heavy chair.
2. Mark moves the chair across from the sofa.
3. Jen doesn't like it there.

Lesson 11

Complete the story. (p. 65)

1. telephone
2. Hello
3. speak
4. wrong
5. rings
6. bother
7. angry
8. number

Check (✔) Yes or No. (p. 66)

1. Yes
2. No
3. Yes
4. No
5. Yes
6. Yes
7. No
8. No
9. No
10. Yes

The Telephone (p. 66)

1. ring
2. pick up
3. hang up

Complete the sentences. (p. 67)

1. rings
2. wakes up
3. picks up
4. asks
5. has
6. hangs up

Listening (p. 68)

A. a. 3
   b. 1
   c. 2
   d. 4

B. 2. 555-0917
   3. 555-3592
   4. 555-7541
   5. 555-9604
   6. 555-3582

Missing Letters (p. 69)

1. bother
2. speak
3. sorry
4. sleeping
5. angry
6. closes
7. telephone
8. number
9. again

Same Sound (p. 69)

2. picks, this
3. answers, asks
4. speak, sleeping
5. you, two

Lesson 12

Complete the story. (p. 71)

1. excited
2. school
3. supplies
4. shopping
5. pencils
6. notebook
7. full
8. teacher

Check (✔) *Yes* or *No*. (p. 72)

1. No
2. No
3. Yes
4. No
5. Yes
6. Yes
7. No
8. Yes
9. Yes
10. No

School Supplies (p. 72)

1. school supplies
2. store
3. shopping basket

Complete the sentences. (p. 73)

1. grade
2. supplies
3. father
4. basket
5. pencils
6. things

Listening (p. 74)

a. 6
b. 1
c. 3
d. 2
e. 4
f. 5

Missing Letters (p. 75)

1. erasers
2. July
3. excited
4. supplies
5. basket
6. teacher
7. September
8. father
9. scissors

Unscramble the sentences. (p. 75)

1. Nadia and her father go to the store.
2. The store has many school supplies.
3. The shopping basket is full.

Lesson 13

Complete the story. (p. 77)
1. son
2. park
3. hill
4. trees
5. swing
6. slide
7. sand
8. Mommy

Check (✔) *Yes* or *No.* (p. 78)
1. Yes
2. No
3. No
4. Yes
5. No
6. No
7. Yes
8. Yes
9. Yes
10. No

Things at the Park (p. 78)
1. slide
2. monkey bars
3. swings

Complete the sentences. (p. 79)
1. takes
2. runs
3. pushes
4. catches
5. helps
6. digs

Listening (p. 80)
a. 4
b. 6
c. 5
d. 1
e. 3
f. 2

Missing Letters (p. 81)
1. a<u>f</u>ternoon
2. sli<u>d</u>e
3. ho<u>l</u>es
4. throu<u>g</u>h
5. do<u>w</u>n
6. mon<u>k</u>ey
7. swi<u>ng</u>
8. ti<u>r</u>ed
9. be<u>h</u>ind

Same Sound (p. 81)
2. three, trees
3. sand, catches
4. takes, okay
5. slide, behind

Lesson 14

Complete the story. (p. 83)
1. music
2. player
3. remote
4. nightstand
5. Power
6. batteries
7. drawer
8. movie

Check (✔) *Yes* or *No.* (p. 84)
1. No
2. No
3. Yes
4. Yes
5. Yes
6. No
7. No
8. Yes
9. No
10. Yes

In Jing's Room (p. 84)
1. batteries
2. CD player
3. remote

Complete the sentences. (p. 85)
1. decides
2. relaxes
3. reaches
4. pushes

5. needs

6. finds

Listening (p. 86)

a. 3

b. 5

c. 4

d. 6

e. 2

f. 1

Missing Letters (p. 87)

1. drawer

2. nightstand

3. music

4. CD player

5. relaxes

6. batteries

7. Power

8. remote

9. button

Unscramble the sentences. (p. 87)

1. He decides to listen to music.

2. This remote needs new batteries.

3. Jing opens the drawer in his nightstand.

Lesson 15

Complete the story. (p. 89)

1. mail

2. form

3. job

4. taxes

5. federal

6. state

7. refund

8. government

Check (✔) *Yes* or *No.* (p. 90)

1. Yes

2. Yes

3. No

4. Yes

5. No

6. No

7. Yes

8. No

9. Yes

10. No

About Income Tax (p. 90)

1. Taxpayer Assistance Center

2. tax refund

3. W-2 form

Complete the sentences. (p. 91)

1. Assistance

2. income

3. state

4. W-2

5. good

6. tax

Listening (p. 92)

A. a. 4

b. 3

c. 2

d. 1

B. 2. $300

3. $400

4. $600

5. $900

6. $500

Missing Letters (p. 93)

1. restaurant

2. state

3. earnings

4. refund

5. government

6. file

7. copy

8. taxpayer

9. federal

Same Sound (p. 93)

2. fill, income

3. owes, shows

4. center, federal

5. earnings, return